WILD GAME

GOURMET STYLE

By

T. J. Burrow

G. W. Teal Publishing Co.

Boise, Idaho

Inexpensive ways to prepare;

Elk, Deer, Antelope, Ducks, Geese,

Pheasants and other upland game birds.

TABLE OF CONTENTS

MARINATED PEPPER VENISON STEAKS

5 medium sized steaks about 1 inch thick
1 1/2 Tsp ground pepper
1/8 cup vegetable oil ;
1/3 cup teriyaki sauce
1/2 cup BBQ sauce of your choice (or brown
sugar and   lemon juice)
1/4 cup red wine
1 oz or 1 shot blended whiskey
1/2 Tsp lemon pepper

**Blend ingredients in a glass or plastic bowl. Add steaks and
let marinate for at least 5 hours. (over night preferably)
Place steaks on the barbecue at a medium high
temperature. Baste steaks with the leftover marinade sauce
before you flip steaks , then cook about 5 more minuets on other side ,**

let rest 3 to 4 minuets.

STEW DELUXE

1 ½ to 2   lbs venison meat (cubed)
1 cup red wine
1 TBSP sea salt
1 1/2 TSP parsley flakes
1/2 TSP pepper
1/2 TBSP lemon juice
1½ cup water

Mix the above ingredients in a crock pot and simmer on high setting for 1 hour. Then add the following ingredient to the crock pot.

2 1/2 cups hot water
4 green onions (sliced)
1/2 cup onion (sliced)
2 carrots (sliced)
3 large mushrooms (sliced)
1 cup broccoli
1 cup cauliflower
1 pinch sage

Cook on med high setting for 1 ½ to 2 more hours.

ANTELOPE

Ground Antelope

Jerky

Meatloaf

Roast

Roast (crock pot style)

Steaks

Steaks (oven style)

Stew

GOOSE

Baked goose

Finger Steaks

Glazed goose

Jerky

Sweet and Sour goose

DUCK

Duck and mushrooms

Glazed Duck over Rice

Smoked Duck Jerky

Finger Steaks

Wild Stir Fry

UPLAND GAME BIRDS

BBQ Sauce

Pheasant and Noodles

Pheasant Strips

Sage Hen and Potatoes

Deep Fried Sage Hen

INTRODUCTION

Through out the **35 years** of my hunting experiences, I have tried many ways to fix and prepare wild game birds and big game.

I have compiled these easy to use gourmet recipes through out my hunting years from trial and error efforts to acquire the most from wild meats. I think with the recipes in this book you will enjoy inexpensive ways to prepare gourmet dishes using your wild game.

Wild game is very delicious if prepared and cooked properly. It is not always cooked and prepared the same as domestic meats. The taste **wild game** offers is based largely upon how it is treated from the field to the freezer. Using the ideas and recipes found in this book you can acquire the most from your wild game.

I hope you try these recipes and find them as enjoyable and delicious as I do.

Simple Pointers on Field Dressing Big Game

Some simple pointers on how to clean deer, antelope and even elk can make a big difference in the flavor of the meat.

After making a quick clean kill, gut and clean the animal as quickly as possible. Place hind quarters of the animal at a higher level than the head, this will aide the bleeding process and allow the intestines to fall into the chest cavity. First cut the throat, then cut the abdomen being careful not to cut any of the intestines. Once the abdomen has been opened, turn the animal so that the hind quarters are lowest, this will permit the intestines and blood to flow out more easily. Next remove all scent glands. When hunting be sure to have a jug of fresh water on hand to clean knife, hands, and any other items that the meat might contact. **WASH HANDS AND KNIFE THOROUGHLY <u>BEFORE</u> SKINNING OR TOUCHING ANY MEAT.** If at all possible, remove skin within 45 minutes of kill so meat can cool quickly. **LEAVE SKIN ON IF YOU MUST DRAG THE ANIMAL TO YOUR VEHICLE.**

Hang meat in cool place below 48 degrees if possible. Wash down with cold water and wrap with wet sheet or thin cloth to keep outer layer of meat from drying out. Cut and wrap meat in proportion to your families' needs.

I always cut meat off bones within 24 hours or as soon as it has cooled completely. Deer and antelope do not have to hang for a long time because their meat does not contain a lot of fat that needs to break down.

DEER RECIPES

VENISON FINGER STEAKS (OVEN STILE)

2 lb venison (sliced into 1/2 inch strips)
1/4 cup Worcestershire sauce
1/3 cup teriyaki sauce •
1/3 cup red wine
1/2 TSP lemon pepper
½ TSP   sea salt

Mix the above ingredients with meat strips in a glass or plastic bowl for at least 12 hours.

Mix in a separate bowl mix the following ingredients.

2 eggs
1/3 cup milk
1/2 TSP oregano (crushed)
1/3 TSP sea salt
1/3 TSP pepper
1/3 TSP sage (crushed)

Remove the strips from the marinade and dab off with a paper towel. Dip strips in the combined egg mixture. Roll and press the meat in 3 cups crushed crackers or croutons crumbs. Place on a cookie sheet and bake at 350 degrees for 35 to 45 minutes. For the last few minutes place the oven on broil to brown. If a crunchy crust is desired,

(Watch carefully on broil)

GROUND VENISON

For every 5 lbs of venison pieces to be ground add the following ingredients.

1 ½ lb pork sausage spicy or plain
1 TBSP lemon pepper
1 TSP garlic salt
1 ½ TBSP sea salt
1 1/2 Tsp cajun mix (optional)
1 ½ TSP crushed red peppers (optional)

Sprinkle the above ingredients over the venison pieces. Combine the 5 lbs of CHILLED venison and 1 ½ lb pork sausage evenly while grinding. (Chilled meat grinds more easily.

If desired you can grind the meat twice to achieve a finer texture. Wrap and freeze in desired quantity.

DEER JERKY

Combine the following ingredients in a large glass or plastic bowl or container.

4 Ibs deer strips or pieces 1/2 inch thick (with the excess fat removed)
1 1/2 cup red wine
1/2 cup sugar "white"
1 1/2 cup brown sugar
3 1/2 TBSPs Kosher salt
2 TBSPs lemon pepper
1 1/2 cups teriyaki sauce
Cold water (to submerge all deer pieces)

Mix ingredients well, add 4 lbs of deer strips or pieces. Let meat marinate for approximately 48 hours in the refrigerator, stir or shake occasionally.

Place strips on smoker rack at 195 to 225 degrees , sprinkle 2 1/2 TBSPs of ground pepper over meat. I use the cherry wood chips, leave on until desired dryness occurs. Usually 3 to 4 hours.

MEAT LOAF

1 1/2 to 2 lbs of ground venison
1 egg
1/3 TSP pepper
2 slices of bread (shredded) or croutons
1/3 cup Worcestershire sauce
1/2 cup onion (diced)
5 long green onion
1 TBSP parsley flakes
1/2 TSP lemon pepper
1 TSP sage
1 TSP oregano
1 ½ TSP sea salt

Combine and mix the above ingredients. Mold into the baking dish and bake for 45 minutes to 1 hour at 350 degrees. Remove the lid and brown for the last 10 minutes, if desired. Salt and pepper to taste.

CROCK POT ROAST

First lightly salt all sides roast with sea salt, then pre heat frying pan with 1/3 cup olive oil Place roast in large pan to sear roast on all sides to brown ,

3 to **4 lb** venison roast
1 cup red wine
1/3 cup teriyaki sauce'
1/2 cup onion (sliced)
4 green onions (sliced)
1 1/2 TSP sea salt
1/2 bay leaf
1 TSP parsley flakes
1/4 TSP sage
1/2 TSP pepper
1 clove garlic (mashed)
2 cups baby mushrooms (whole)
3 to 4 cups water

Place roast in a crock pot with the above ingredients over the roast, Slow Cook on high setting for 4 to 4 ½ hours (depending on the roast size). Add the mushrooms 1/2 hour before the roast is done. Use the juice for a great tasting gravy.

VENISON ROAST

3 to 4 lb roast
1/2 medium onion, quartered
1/3 Tsp ground pepper
1/2 Tsp sea salt
1/2 cup red wine
1 garlic clove (mashed)
2 1/2 pinches crushed oregano
1 pinch sage
1 1/2 cups water

Brown roast in skillet with garlic clove and 1 1/2 TBSP butter. Place in baking dish, pour the water and wine over roast. Sprinkle remaining ingredients over the roast.

Place roast in the oven at 350 degrees for 2 1/2 to 3 1/2 hours. (Depends on the size of roast.) Add potatoes and other vegetables 50 minutes before the roast is done.

WILD STIR FRY - VENISON

Prepare rice before hand, in the amount desired.

1 lb. venison, cubed
1 1/2 cup broccoli
1/2 cup cauliflower
1/3 cup soy sauce
1 tsp. butter
1/2 cup tomatoes, cubed
1/3 cup white wine
1/3 tsp. pepper
1 TBSP lemon juice
4 green onions, sliced
1/3 cup Teriyaki sauce

Brown meat in large skillet or wok, with butter and lemon uice. Add cooked rice to meat and fry for 5 to 10 minutes on med hi heat, stirring frequently. Add remaining ingredients to skillet. Cover and let reduce heat to low , simmer for 10 minutes.

ELK RECIPES

ELK CROCK POT ROAST

3 to 4 lb elk roast
1 cup red wine
1/3 cup teriyaki sauce
1/2 cup onion (sliced)
4 green onions (sliced)
1 1/2 TSP sea salt
1/2 bay leaf
1 TSP parsley flakes
1/4 TSP sage
1/2 TSP pepper
1 clove garlic (mashed)
2 large mushrooms (sliced)
1 1/2 to 2 cups water
2 to 4 medium potatoes cut up
2 to 4 carrots sliced

Place roast in a crock pot with the above ingredients over the roast, except the vegetables. Cook on high setting for 2 to 3 hours (depending on the roast size). Add the vegetables , cook for another hour until vegetables are done. Use the juice for a great tasting gravy.

GROUND ELK

For every 5 lbs of elk pieces to be ground , add the following ingredients.

1 1/2 lb pork sausage spicy or plain
1/2 TBSPs lemon pepper
1/2 TSP garlic salt
1 TBSP sea salt
1 Tsp cajun mix (optional)
1 TBSP Crushed red peppers (optional)

Sprinkle the above ingredients over the elk pieces. Combine the 5 lbs of CHILLED elk and 1 1/2 lb pork sausag ,evenly while grinding. (Chilled meat grinds more easily.) If desired you can add a garlic clove and grind in with meat ,

Wrap and freeze in desired quantity.

ELK JERKY

Combine the following ingredients in a large glass or plastic bowl or container. Always use plastic or glass, (Not Stainless or metal, can taint meat with the salt reaction)

4 to 5 lbs elk strips or pieces 1/2 inch thick (with the excess fat removed)
1 1/2 cup red wine
1 1/2 cup sugar brown
1 TBSPs sea salt
1 TBSPs lemon pepper
2 TBSPs ground pepper
1 1/2 cups teriyaki sauce
2 cups cold water (if needed to cover deer pieces)

Mix ingredients well, add 4 to 5 lbs of elk strips or pieces. Let meat marinate for approximately 48 hours in the refrigerator, stir or shake occasionally. Place strips on smoker rack, at 185 degrees for about 1 ½ hours , sprinkle 2 TBSPs of ground pepper over meat.
Finish smoking at about 225 degrees, until desired dryness occurs. I like to use cherry wood chips.

ELK MEAT LOAF

1 1/2 to 2 1/2 lbs of ground elk
1 egg
1/3 TSP pepper
2 slices of bread (shredded) or crushed croutons
1/3 cup Worcestershire sauce
1/2 cup onion (diced)
1 TBSP parsley flakes
1/2 TSP lemon pepper
1 to 2 pinches sage
1 to 2 pinches oregano
3 TBSP ketchup
2 TBSP horse radish sauce

Combine and mix the above ingredients. Mold into the baking dish and bake for 1 ½ hour at 350 degrees. Remove the lid and brown for the last 10 minutes, if desired. Salt and pepper to taste.

ELK ROAST

4 to 6 lb roast
1 medium onion (quartered)
1/2 Tsp ground pepper
1 Tsp sea salt
2/3 cup red wine
1 clove
2 1/2 pinches crushed oregano
1 1/2 pinches sage
1 1/2 cups water
2 garlic clove (mashed)

Salt roast lightly then brown roast in skillet with garlic clove and 2 TBSP butter or olive oil

Place in baking dish, pour the water and wine over roast. Sprinkle remaining ingredients over the roast. Place roast in oven af 350 degrees for 2 1/2 to 3 1/2 hours, depending upon the roast size. Add potatoes and vegetables, and bake for an additional 45 minutes.

MARINATED ELK STEAKS

2 large sized elk steaks about 1 inch thick
1/2 Tsp ground pepper
1/8 cup vegetable oil
1/3 cup teriyaki sauce
1/2 cup BBQ sauce of your choice
1/4 cup red wine
1 oz or 1 shot blended whiskey
1/2 Tsp lemon pepper

Blend ingredients in a glass or plastic bowl. Add steaks and let marinate for at least 5 hours. (over night preferably) Place steaks on the barbecue at a medium high temperature. Baste steaks with the leftover marinade sauce until done.

ELK FINGER STEAKS (OVEN STYLE)

1 lb elk (sliced into 1/2 inch strips)
1/4 cup worcestershire sauce
1/3 cup teriyaki sauce
1/3 cup red wine
1/2 TSP lemon pepper

Mix the above ingredients with meat strips in a glass or plastic bowl for at least 12 hours.

Mix in a separate bowl the following ingredients.

2 eggs
1/3 cup milk
1/2 TSP oregano (crushed)
1/2 TSP Sea Salt

Remove the strips from the marinade and dab off with a paper towel. Dip strips in the combined egg mixture. Press the meat in 3 cups crushed crackers or croutons crumbs. Place on a cookie sheet and bake at 350 degrees for 35 to 45 minutes. For the last few minutes place the oven on broil to brown. (Watch carefully on broil)

CHUNKY ELK STEW

1 1/2 lbs elk meat (cubed)
1 cup red wine
1 TBSP kosher or sea salt
1 1/2 TSP parsley flakes
1/2 TSP pepper
1/2 TBSP lemon juice
1/2 TSP Oregano

Mix the above ingredients in a crock pot and simmer on high setting for 1 hour. Then add the following ingredients to the crock pot.

1 pinch sage
3 1/2 cups hot water
4 green onions (sliced)
1/2 cup onion (sliced)
2 carrots (sliced)
3 large mushrooms (sliced)
1 1/2 cup broccoli
1 cup cauliflower

Cook on high setting in slow cooker for 3 1/2 to 4 hours.

ANTELOPE RECIPES

GROUND ANTELOPE

For every 3 1bs of antelope pieces to be ground add the following ingredients.

1 lb pork sausage spicy or plain
1/2 TBSPs lemon pepper
1/2 TSP garlic salt
1 TBSP sea salt
1 Tsp cajun mix (optional)
1/3 cup brown sugar

Sprinkle the above ingredients over the antelope pieces. Combine the 3 lbs of chilled antelope and 1 lb pork sausage evenly while grinding. Chilled meat grinds more easily. If desired you can grind the meat twice to achieve a finer texture. Wrap and freeze in desired quantity.

ANTELOPE JERKY

Combine the following ingredients in a large glass or plastic bowl or container.

4 lbs antelope strips or pieces 1/2 inch thick (with the excess fat removed)
1 1/2 cup red wine
1/2 cup sugar "white"
3 TBSPs kosher salt
1 1/2 TBSPs lemon pepper
1/2 cup brown sugar
1 cup worcestershire sauce
2 cups cold water (if needed to cover deer pieces)
2 TSPs red crushed pepper (if you like it hotter)

Mix ingredients well, add 4 lbs of antelope strips or pieces. Let meat marinate for approximately 48 hours in the refrigerator, stir or shake occasionally. Place strips on smoker rack, sprinkle 2 TBSPs of ground pepper over meat. Smoke with cherry wood chips at about 195 degrees until desired dryness occurs.

MEATLOAF

1 1/2 to 2 lbs of ground antelope
1 egg
1/3 TSP pepper
2 slices of bread (shredded)
1/3 cup worcestershire sauce
1/2 cup onion (diced)
1 TBSP parsley flakes
1/2 TSP lemon pepper
1 to 2 pinches sage
1 to 2 pinches oregano
1 TBSP ketchup

Combine and mix the above ingredients. Mold into the baking dish and bake for 45 minutes to 1 hour at 350 degrees. Remove the lid and brown for the last 15 minutes if desired. Salt and pepper to taste.

ANTELOPE ROAST

3 4 lb roast
1 medium onion, quartered
1 Tsp ground pepper
1 Tsp sea salt
1 cup red wine
1 garlic clove (mashed)
1/2 pinches crushed oregano
1 inch sage
1/2 cups water.

Brown roast in skillet on all sides with garlic clove and 1/3 cup olive oil. Place in baking dish, pour the water and wine over roast. Sprinkle remaining ingredients over the roast.

Place roast in the oven at 350 degrees for 2 1/2 to 3 1/2 hours. (Depends on the size of roast.) Add potatoes and other vegetables 50 minutes before the roast is done.

CROCK POT ROAST

2 1/2 to 4 lb antelope roast
1 cup red wine
1/3 cup teriyaki sauce
1/2 cup onion (sliced)
4 green onions (sliced)
1 1/2 TSP sea salt
1/2 bay leaf
1 TSP parsley flakes
1/4 TSP sage
1/2 TSP pepper
1 clove garlic (mashed)
2 large mushrooms (sliced)
1 1/2 to 2 cups water
2 cups broccoli
2 to 4 carrots

Place roast in a crock pot with the above ingredients ov
the roast, except the vegetables. Cook on high setting fo
1/2 to 4 hours (depending on the roast size). Add the
vegetables 1 hour before the roast is done (potatoes i
desired). Use the juice for a great tasting gravy.

MARINATED ANTELOPE STEAKS

5 medium sized steaks about 1 inch thick
1/3 Tsp ground pepper
1/8 cup vegetable oil
1/3 cup teriyaki sauce
1/2 cup BBQ sauce of your choice
1/4 cup red wine
1 oz or 1 shot blended whiskey
1/2 Tsp lemon pepper

**Blend ingredients in a glass or plastic bowl. Add steaks and
let marinate for at least 5 hours. (over night preferably)**

**Place steaks on the barbecue at a medium high
perature, for 5 minuets. Baste steaks with the leftover marinade sauce
ore flipping cook approximately 5 minuets other side, depending how
your BBQ cooks.**

ANTELOPE FINGER STEAKS (OVEN STYLE)

1 lb antelope (sliced into 1/2 inch strips)
1/4 cup worcestershire' sauce
1/3 cup teriyaki sauce
1/3 cup red wine
1/2 TSP lemon pepper

Mix the above ingredients with meat strips in a glass or plastic bowl for at least 12 hours.

Mix in a separate bowl the following ingredients.

2 eggs
1/3 cup milk
1/2 TSP oregano (crushed)
1/2 TSP sea salt
1/3 TSP pepper
1/3 TSP sage (crushed)

Remove the strips from the marinade and dab off with a paper towel. Dip strips in the combined egg mixture. Roll the meat in 3 cups crushed crackers or croutons crumbs. Place on a cookie sheet and bake at 350 degrees for 35 to 40 minutes. For the last few minutes place the oven on broil to brown. (Watch carefully on broil)

ANTELOPE STEW

1 1/2 lbs antelope meat (cubed)
1 cup red wine
1/2 TBSP sea salt
1 1/2 TSP parsley flakes
1/2 TSP pepper
1/2 TBSP lemon juice
1/2 TSP Oregano

Mix the above ingredients in a crock pot and simmer on high setting for 1 hour. Then add the following ingredients to the crock pot.

1 pinch sage
3 1/2 cups hot water
4 green onions (sliced)
1/2 cup onion (sliced)
2 carrots (sliced)
3 large mushrooms (sliced)
1 cup broccoli
1 cup cauliflower

Slow Cook on high setting for

3 1/2 to 4 hours.

GOOSE RECIPE

BAKED GOOSE

ace skinned goose in 9 by 13 glass baking dish. Add 1 cup
d wine over goose. Then sprinkle the following seasonings
over the bird.

1/2 TBSP Cajun mix
1 TSP sea salt
1/2 TBSP Lemon Pepper
1/2 cup onion sliced, place in and over goose
1 pinch sage, sprinkle over goose
1/2 TBSP parsley, sprinkle over goose

Add 2 cups of water to the baking dish. Cover the goose
with foil tightly. Bake at 325 degrees for 3 hours. Baste
rd occasionally. Turn oven to 350 degrees for the last 1/2
n hour of baking time. At this time you can uncover for
browning. Use the juice for a delicious gravy.

GOOSE FINGER STEAKS

Cut both goose breast into 1/2 inch strips.

1/2 cup Worcestershire sauce
1/3 cup red wine
1 1/2 TBSP lemon juice
1/2 tsp pepper
1 tsp parsley
½ TSP SEA SALT

Mix goose strips and above ingredients in large glass or plastic bowl. Marinate for at least 5 hours in refrigerator.

Then mix the following ingredients in a separate bowl.

1 cup flour
1 cup water
1 tsp oregano (crushed)
1 egg
1 tsp lemon pepper
1/2 tsp Sea salt
1/2 tsp garlic salt

Remove meat from marinade sauce and blot with paper towel. Dip in above mixture and fry in hot oil until golden brown.

GLAZED GOOSE

**Marinate 1/2 goose breast (cubed) pieces in 1/3 cup
·iyaki sauce and 1/3 cup red wine for 12 hours if possible,
to enhance the flavor of this recipe.**

1/2 goose breast (cubed)
1/4 cup worcestershire sauce
1/3 cup red wine
1/4 cup catsup
1 TBSP lemon juice
1 TBSP parsley flakes
1/2 garlic clove (mashed)
1 pinch oregano
1 pinch sage
3 green onions (sliced)

**Strain goose from marinade and fry in skillet on medium
gh heat with garlic clove until brown on all sides. Add the
ove ingredients to skillet and simmer until sauce thickens.
Place over wild rice. Salt and pepper to taste.**

SMOKED GOOSE JERKY

Place the following ingredients. in a large glass or plastic bowl. .

1 1/2 TBSP lemon pepper
1 TBSP cajun mix
1 1/2 TSP kosher salt
1/2 cup teriyaki sauce
1 1/2 cup red wine or 1/2 of a beer
1/4 cup sugar "white"
4 cups cold water
1/2 cup brown sugar

Cut 2 goose (breasts) into 1/2 inch strips. Let strips marinate for 24 to 48 hours in the refrigerator.

Place strips on smoker racks,at about 185 degrees, sprinkle 1 TBSP goo pepper
over strips. Smoke meat for approximately six hours, read directions for your particular smoker for jerky since all smokers vary.

SWEET AND SOUR FRIED GOOSE

1/2 goose breast
1/3 cup teriyaki sauce
1 cup sweet and sour sauce
1 1/2 TBSPs parsley flakes
1 pinch sage
3 to 4 green onions (sliced)
1 clove garlic (mashed)
salt and pepper to taste

Cut goose breast into thin slices. Place goose in skillet and fry in 1 TBSP butter and garlic clove until brown or crisp. Add teriyaki sauce and let simmer for a few minutes. Add the remaining ingredients to skillet and stir. Let sauce thicken at medium low heat. Serve over mashed potatoes or rice.

(This same recipe can be used on leftovers from the BAKED GOOSE recipe. It is delicious.)

DUCK

DUCK AND MUSHROOMS

1 large duck breast (slice into cubes)
4 green onions (sliced)
5 large mushrooms (sliced)
1 cup red wine
1/4 cup teriyaki sauce
1 1/2 cups of mixed vegetables, broccoli, carrots, etc.
1/2 cup tomatoes (diced)
2 Tbsp catsup
2 Tsp brown sugar
1 Tspsea salt
1/2 Tsp ground pepper

Marinate duck cubes in 1/2 cup wine and 1/2 cup teriyaki sauce for about 12 hours. Strain duck cubes from marinade and brown in skillet on all sides for 5 to 10 minutes.

ld the above ingredients with duck. Cover and let simmer for 10 to 15 minutes, remove lid and let thicken. Place over rice or mashed potatoes. Salt and pepper to taste.

GLAZED DUCK OVER RICE

Marinate 1 duck breast (cubed) pieces in 1/3 cup teriyaki sauce and 1/3 cup red wine for 12 hours if possible, to enhance the flavor of this recipe.

1 duck breast (cubed)
1/4 cup worcestershire sauce
1/3 cup red wine
1/4 cup catchup
1 TBSP lemon juice
1 TBSP parsley flakes
1/2 garlic clove (mashed)
1 pinch oregano
1 pinch sage
3 green onions (sliced)

Strain duck from marinade and fry in skillet on medium high heat with garlic clove until brown on all sides. Add th above ingredients to skillet and simmer until sauce thicken. Place over wild rice. Salt and pepper to taste.

SMOKED DUCK JERKY

Place the following ingredients in a large glass or plastic bowl.

1 TBSP lemon pepper
1/2 TBSP cajun mix
1 TBSP kosher salt
1/2 cup teriyaki sauce
1 1/2 cups red wine or 1 beer
1/3 cup sugar "white"
1 cup cold water (if needed to cover meat)
1/2 cup brown sugar

Cut 3 to 4 duck breasts into 1/3 inch strips. Let strips marinate for 24 to 48 hours in the refrigerator. Mix or shake occasionally.

Place strips on smoker rack, sprinkle 1 TBSP ground pepper over strips. Let meat smoke for approximately six hours, and directions for your particular smoker since all smokers vary.

DUCK FINGER STEAKS

Cut two duck breasts into 1/2 inch strips.

1/2 cup Worcestershire sauce
1/3 cup red wine
1 1/2 TBSP lemon juice

Mix duck strips and above ingredients in large glass or . plastic bowl. Marinate for at least 24 hours in refrigerator

Then mix the following ingredients in a separate bowl:

1 cup flour
1 cup water
1 TSP oregano (crushed)
1 egg
1 TSP lemon pepper
1 TSP sea salt

Remove meat from marinade sauce and blot with paper towel. Dip in above mixture and fry in hot oil until golden brown.

WILD STIR FRY - DUCK

Marinate 2 cups, boneless, cubed duck meat over night in
1/3 cup Worcestershire sauce and 1/3 cup red wine.
Prepare rice before hand, in the amount desired.

1 ½ to 2 lb venison, cubed
1 1/2 cup broccoli
1/2 cup cauliflower
1/3 cup soy sauce
1 tsp; butter
1/2 cup tomatoes, cubed
1/3 cup white wine
1/3 tsp, pepper
1 TBSP lemon juice
4 green onions, sliced
1/3 cup Teriyaki sauce

Remove meat from marinade sauce and brown in large
skillet or wok, with butter and lemon juice. Add cooked
rice to meat and fry for 5 to 10 minutes, stirring frequently.

Add remaining ingredients to skillet. Cover and let simmer
for 10 minutes.

UPLAND GAME BIRDS

BBQ SAUCE FOR UPLAND GAME BIRDS

This is an excellent sauce to baste over pheasants , quail, sage hen grouse , forest grouse and doves, just to name a few.

2 to 4 upland game birds (preferably skinned and boneless)
1/3 cup olive oil
1/4 cup ketchup
1/3 cup worcestershire
1/2 TSP sea salt
1/3 TSP sage (crushed)
2 green onions (sliced finely)
2 TBSP   brown sugar
1 shot blended whiskey

**all above ingredients well . Turn barbecuer to medium heat and place birds on barbecue for 10 minutes on each side.
en birds start to brown, start to baste birds with sauce. Continue cooking and basting birds until golden brown or completely done. Sauce will brown along with birds.**

PHEASANT AND NOODLES

1 pheasant - breast, legs, and thighs
2 TBSP oliveoil
1/2 cup onions (chopped)
5 or 6 green onions (chopped)
1 TSP pepper
2 TBSP Worcestershire sauce
1 ½ TSP sea salt
1/2 TBSP fresh sage
1 garlic clove (finely chopped)
2 TBSP dry parsley flakes
3 to 4 cups water to cover bird
1 package of egg noodles
1/3 cup chopped cilantro

Place pheasant and the above ingredients in a crock pot and slow cook on high heat for 2 hours. Use slotted spoon to remove pheasant from crock pot. Remove the meat from the bones (the meat should fall off the bone easily).

Place meat back into the crock pot and add your choice of egg nood Cook for 25 to 35 minutes or until the noodles are tender. This is excellent over mashed potatoes.

PHEASANT STRIPS (OVEN STYLE)

**Cut 2 skinless pheasants breasts into 1 1/2 inch strips.
Combine the following ingredients in a mixing bowl.**

1/2 TSP sage (crushed)

1 TSP sea salt
2 eggs
1/2 TSP fresh oregano
1/3 cup **milk**
1/2 TSP cajun seasoning (optional)

**Dip the pheasant strips into the bowl with the above
ingredients. Then press the strips into 2 1/2 cups of crushed
ackers crumbs or crushed croutons. Place strips on a cookie sheet and
bake at 350 degrees for 45 minutes. You may want to turn
the oven to broil for the last 3 or 4 minutes of baking time for
browning, if desired. (Watch carefully on broil)**

SAGEHEN AND POTATOES

or

FOREST GROUSE

1 sagehen breast (cut into 1/2 inch cubes)
2 medium potatoes (cut into 1/2 inch cubes or
thin strips)
1¼ cup vegetable oil
1/2 TSP sea salt
1/2 cup onion (diced)
3 green onions (diced)
2 TSP fresh parsley flakes
3 or 4 large mushrooms slices

Heat oil in large skillet on medium high heat. Then add the
potatoes to the skillet, fry for 10 minuets, then add the sage h
or grouse meat and and fry on medium high,until meat is
browned

Reduce heat to medium and
then add the remaining ingredients to the skillet and cover ar
let cook
until potatoes are done.

DEEP FRIED SAGEHEN SANDWICH

is is a great way to prepare sagehen when your in the
esert for the weekend hunting for the little critters.

Take along these items:' coleman stove, large pot.

And olive oil

oz vegetable oil , or olive oil
salt
yonnaise
seradish sauce
atoes
ad
TSUP

**Slice your sage hen and potatoes into thin strips and place in
hot oil, deep fry until golden brown. Place mayonnaise,
horseradish and sage hen strips on your bread.**

**Sprinkle a
little of your favorite Seasonings over your potatoes and
sandwich for added flavor.**

**Enjoy a simple and great tasting
meal!!**

Manufactured by Amazon.ca
Bolton, ON

10400377R00030